Original title:
The Silver Veil

Copyright © 2024 Creative Arts Management OÜ
All rights reserved.

Author: Rafael Sterling
ISBN HARDBACK: 978-9916-88-880-3
ISBN PAPERBACK: 978-9916-88-881-0

Glimmers of Hidden Journeys

In the shadows, whispers call,
Footsteps echo, soft and small.
Paths unseen, where secrets roam,
Hearts ignite, they find their home.

Stars align in distant skies,
Trust the compass, hear the sighs.
Winds of change begin to blow,
In the dark, the embers glow.

Lace of Luminescent Memories

Threads of time, they weave and wind,
Fleeting moments, softly bind.
Ghosts of laughter, shades of gold,
In each heartbeat, stories told.

Held in dreams, where echoes play,
Bright reflections of yesterday.
Kaleidoscope of joy and pain,
In our hearts, the lace remains.

The Shimmering Boundary of Dreams

In twilight's grasp, realities blend,
Silent wishes like rivers bend.
Between the stars and earthly sighs,
Hope takes flight on feathered skies.

Veils of slumber, gently part,
Casting light upon the heart.
Whispers trickle, soft and bright,
Guiding souls through endless night.

Eclipsed by Glistening Grace

Moonbeams dance on silver streams,
Closet of nighttime, filled with dreams.
Touched by grace, the shadows play,
In the dawn, they drift away.

Each tear sparkles, each laugh glows,
In the silence, true love knows.
Time may fade, yet still we chase,
Each embrace, a glistening grace.

Threads of Mysterious Delicacy

In shadows spun from whispered dreams,
The night weaves tales with silver seams.
Fragile strands of laughter burst,
In delicate moments, we trust.

Beneath the moon's soft, watchful gaze,
Secrets dance in a shimmering haze.
Each thread a promise, soft and bright,
Binding hearts in the tender light.

Woven gently, the stories flow,
Carrying hopes where wildflowers grow.
In the tapestry of time, we find,
A thread of love, intricately aligned.

From silken whispers to gentle sighs,
Mysteries linger under distant skies.
Each delicate stitch, a memory spun,
In the fabric of life, we're never done.

Swaying under the Pastel Night

Dreams wander softly in twilight's embrace,
Colors blend, painting the sky's face.
Stars twinkle like whispers in flight,
Swaying gently under pastel night.

The breeze carries echoes of laughter clear,
Chasing away shadows, drawing us near.
Underneath the canopy of soft light,
We sway together, hearts feeling right.

Each moment a dance, a step, a sway,
Painting the world in hues of the day.
With each breath, the night sings a tune,
As we sway beneath the watching moon.

In this tranquil space, our spirits unite,
Lost in the magic of the gentle night.
With pastel skies and dreams set free,
Together we dance, just you and me.

Hushed Echoes of Radiant Secrets

In shadows deep, where whispers play,
The secrets dance, they softly sway.
With every breath, a tale unfolds,
In hushed echoes, the truth beholds.

Beneath the stars, a night divine,
Radiant dreams in darkness shine.
The heart's soft pulse, a gentle tune,
In silent nights, we commune with the moon.

Where time stands still, and thoughts take flight,
In the warmth of love, all feels right.
With every sigh, a spark ignites,
In hushed echoes of starry nights.

The secrets held in quiet grace,
In the tapestry of time and space.
With every heartbeat, stories blend,
In radiant whispers, we transcend.

Reflections on a Misted Surface

Upon the lake, where silence weaves,
Reflections dance among the leaves.
Misted surface, a secret pond,
Where fleeting moments gently respond.

A whispering breeze, the ripples play,
Carrying thoughts that drift away.
In gentle swirls, the memories blend,
On misty waves, the echoes send.

The sun peers through, a golden beam,
Illuminates a fragile dream.
Each glance reveals a hidden story,
In mirrored depths, we seek the glory.

With every turn, new visions bloom,
In the soft embrace of nature's room.
Reflections speak of times long past,
On a misted surface, peace is cast.

Moonlight's Embrace of Illumination

In silver beams, the night takes flight,
Moonlight wraps the world in light.
A luminous path where shadows fade,
In gentle glow, our dreams are made.

The whispers of the midnight air,
Breathe secrets soft, beyond compare.
Every star, a guiding spark,
In moonlight's arms, we leave our mark.

With every glance, the heart ignites,
A dance of souls in starry nights.
In tender glow, we find our way,
Through moonlit paths, forever stay.

Each moment captured, a sweet embrace,
In moonlight's warmth, we find our place.
Where love prevails, and shadows cease,
In tranquility, our hearts find peace.

Veiled in Radiant Emotions

Beneath the veil of silken dreams,
Radiant emotions flow like streams.
In soft whispers, hearts intertwine,
The tapestry of love, so divine.

With every heartbeat, colors bloom,
Painting the air with sweet perfume.
In vibrant hues, our spirits soar,
Veiled in magic, forevermore.

Like autumn leaves, we drift and sway,
In luminous dance, we laugh and play.
Emotions rise like tides at sea,
In radiant currents, we are free.

With each tender touch, the world ignites,
Veiled in love's glow, we reach new heights.
In rhythms of life, our souls ignite,
In radiant emotions, we find our light.

Ethereal Woven Silhouettes

In whispers soft, the shadows play,
Echoes dance on twilight's sway.
Figures form in night's embrace,
Ethereal threads weave through space.

Fleeting forms in silver light,
Framed in dreams of endless night.
Glimmers fade as dawn draws near,
Silhouettes of what once was here.

Veils of Night and Stardust

Veils of night draped overhead,
Stars like whispers softly spread.
Beneath the vast and velvet sky,
Eons pass, as constellations lie.

Waves of stardust shimmer bright,
Guiding hearts through depths of night.
In the silence, secrets bloom,
Veils of wonder chase the gloom.

The Enigma of Soft Radiance

Within the glow of gentle beams,
Mysteries woven through our dreams.
Soft radiance caresses skin,
Illuminating worlds within.

Fleeting moments, time stands still,
A tender touch, a silent thrill.
In every glimmer, truth does hide,
The enigma where hopes abide.

Ghostly Hues of Enchantment

Ghostly hues in twilight's gaze,
Shadows linger, soft and maze.
Whispers call from woods so deep,
Secrets shared that shadows keep.

Colors blend in muted light,
Enchanting forms that twist in flight.
In spectral dances, spirits twine,
A haunting thread of the divine.

Canvas of the Unseen

In hues of night, the stars do dance,
Silent whispers, caught in a trance.
Each brushstroke glows with a hidden tale,
A dreamlike realm, where shadows sail.

Color blends with thoughts unspoken,
The canvas breathes, its heart unbroken.
A vision blooms, yet stays concealed,
A tapestry of truths revealed.

Veil of Forgotten Time

Memories weave through the mists of years,
Silent echoes, laughter, and tears.
Ancient stories lie beneath the stone,
A veil draped softly, forever known.

Time's gentle hands brush through the past,
Whispers linger, shadows are cast.
The clock ticks slowly, yet speeds away,
In this forgotten, wistful ballet.

Whispers of Luminous Elegance

Golden rays touch petals with grace,
Nature's art in a warm embrace.
Glistening lights through emerald leaves,
A symphony of beauty, heart perceives.

Softly shimmering in twilight's glow,
The world awakens with vibrant flow.
Delicate sighs from blossoms draw near,
In this realm, all doubts disappear.

Shadows in Gossamer Dreams

In floating veils, the night unfolds,
Whispers of dreams, in silence told.
Shadows dance with the moon's soft light,
Enigmas wane, lost to the night.

With every breath, a secret sways,
Gossamer threads in the silver haze.
Reality blurs, and hopes ascend,
In this twilight world, where dreams blend.

Cascading Silvers of Forgotten Stories

Whispers dance on aged leaves,
Tales entwined in silken threads,
Breezes carry echoes far,
The past in twilight spreads.

Moonlight bathes the silent streams,
Memory's touch, a gentle call,
Every ripple softly gleams,
Reflecting dreams of all.

Stars align in secret ways,
Mapping journeys yet to unfold,
Under skies where hope still plays,
And warmth resides in the cold.

In shadows where the stories dwell,
Cascading silvers take their flight,
Telling secrets, weaving spells,
Embraced by the silent night.

Laced with Celestial Essence

The dawn wraps light in golden lace,
Celestial whispers fill the air,
Each sunbeam finds a hidden place,
Where dreams and daylight dare.

Stars adorn the night in grace,
Carving paths in velvet skies,
Glimmers trace the time's embrace,
Awakening hopeful sighs.

Moonlit tales in stillness spun,
Laced with essence of the night,
Every moment just begun,
Enveloped in soft twilight.

In the silence, souls align,
Celestial bodies, pure and bright,
Drawing hearts with love divine,
Together in the endless flight.

The Sheen of Transcendent Visions

From shadows rise the visions clear,
Glimmers dance in vibrant hues,
Echoes of a world sincere,
Beneath the light, hope renews.

Through the mist of dreams untold,
Whispers glisten like the rain,
Transcendent beauty, brave and bold,
In every joy, there's no pain.

Beyond the realms of dusk and dawn,
The sheen of what truly gleams,
In the heart, the light is drawn,
Illuminating tender dreams.

Cascading colors fill the space,
Soft reflections of the soul,
In the dance of time and grace,
Transcendence makes the spirit whole.

Enfolded in Shining Shadows

Shadows weave through timeless nights,
Embracing silence, soft and deep,
In the dance of hidden lights,
Whispers where the secrets sleep.

Nightfall cloaks the world in peace,
Each shimmer fades into the dark,
Yet from silence comes release,
A promise held within the spark.

Enfolded in the gentle breeze,
Shining shadows grace the land,
In the stillness, find your ease,
Together as we take a stand.

Hearts entwined in twilight's glow,
Finding joy in every sigh,
In the shadows, love will grow,
As stars weave dreams across the sky.

Luminous Mirage

In desert nights the shadows play,
A glowing path where dreamers sway,
Mirages dance in shimmering light,
Whispers of hope in the quiet night.

Stars above, like diamonds gleam,
Guiding lost souls toward a dream,
Each flicker a promise, soft and bright,
Trust the journey, embrace the flight.

The wind's sweet song fills the air,
Tales of wonder hidden there,
With every step, a chance awaits,
In the heart of fate, love resonates.

A luminous path beneath our feet,
Echoes of laughter, a soft heartbeat,
In the mirage, we find our way,
Together we'll shine at the break of day.

Secrets of the Moonlight

Moonlight spills on silver waves,
Casting dreams with light it saves,
Each beam holds whispers of the night,
Secrets woven, pure and bright.

Underneath the guiding glow,
Stories from the ancients flow,
In shadows deep, the truth awaits,
Unlocked by love, it illuminates.

A soft embrace of twilight's kiss,
In each soft sigh, we find our bliss,
With every secret shared in trust,
Hearts align, a magical lust.

Beneath the stars, we dare to roam,
In moonlit dreams, we find our home,
Together we dance through realms unknown,
In this sacred space, love has grown.

Veil Between Worlds

A veil hangs softly, thin and sheer,
Between the realms, what draws us near?
Mysteries cloak the quiet space,
Where time and dreams find their place.

Each flutter whispers secrets old,
Of tales untold, of hearts so bold,
Through the veil, we glimpse and see,
The echoes of what used to be.

In the stillness, we wander slow,
Where shadows dance and moonbeams flow,
Guided by hope and tender light,
We bridge the gap between day and night.

Together we step beyond the line,
Unraveling paths where our souls entwine,
In the veil, a promise we twirl,
In silence, we craft our secret world.

Celestial Cloak

Worn like a dream, the stars align,
In the celestial cloak, we find the divine,
Each stitch a story, a moment's grace,
Woven with love, in time's embrace.

Galaxies sway in the fabric of night,
Painting our hearts with shimmering light,
Through cosmic dances, we weave our fate,
In the cloak of the heavens, we softly wait.

A tapestry rich with colors bold,
Of adventures shared and secrets untold,
In every thread, a memory glows,
The warmth of eternity, as love flows.

As we journey beneath the bright sky,
Wrapped in stardust, together we fly,
With each heartbeat, the universe sings,
In the celestial cloak, we are king and queen.

Pastel Glimmers of Subdued Dreams

In twilight's embrace, colors blend soft,
Whispers of visions hang lightly aloft.
Gentle hues dance, as shadows recede,
Carrying secrets of hearts set to heed.

Moments suspended, where silence holds sway,
Soft laughter echoes, drifting away.
Drenched in the past, yet eager to soar,
Embracing the solace that dreams can explore.

Velvet skies shimmer with hints of the dawn,
Pastel glimmers trace the paths that we've drawn.
As mystique lingers, unfurling like wings,
A canvas of hopes, where the night softly sings.

Bathed in the light of all we once known,
Each brushstroke of memory, carefully sown.
Subdued but alive, our spirits will gleam,
In a world woven tight with the fabric of dreams.

Embracing the Glistening Unknown

Step into the night, where stars softly shine,
The future awaits, so divine, so fine.
With shadows as guides, we'll wander through time,
Embracing the thrill of the unscripted climb.

Each heartbeat a promise, each breath a new start,
To navigate paths drawn by pulse of the heart.
The glimmer of hope lies in every step taken,
Towards horizons unknown, where nothing is shaken.

The dance of the daring, the call of the wild,
With laughter liké music, each moment beguiled.
We chase fleeting dreams, in the still of the dark,
Igniting the fire, igniting the spark.

As we venture forth, hand in hand through the maze,
Life's tapestry woven of unpredictable ways.
In glistening shadows, we forge our own light,
Embracing the unknown, hearts ready for flight.

Enchanted by Halos of Serenity

In gardens of stillness, the breezes conspire,
Soft whispers of peace, a gentle desire.
Halos of calm, like a soft flowing stream,
Enchanted by moments, suspending the dream.

The hush of the dawn, a tender reprieve,
In quiet reflections, we learn how to believe.
With petals unfolding, they greet the new day,
Guided by serenity's comforting sway.

With each breath we take, we anchor our souls,
In still waters deep, where the heart gently rolls.
Wrapped in the warmth of this tranquil embrace,
Time dances with grace in this sacred space.

As we linger in silence, the world fades away,
Cherishing whispers that softly convey:
A symphony sweet, in the heart's gentle plea,
Enchanted forever, in halos of serenity.

Fragments of Elysian Mystique

In twilight's soft glow, where magic resides,
Fragments of wonder drift where love abides.
A whisper of history brushed with pure light,
Elysian dreams dance in the folds of the night.

Each moment a treasure, each echo a song,
Where lost souls gather, where we all belong.
Mystique swirls around in a veil ever thin,
Embracing the shadows, letting dreams in.

The stars bear witness to the tales yet untold,
Unlocking the secrets that the heavens hold.
In gardens of wonder, our spirits take flight,
Reflecting the beauty concealed from the sight.

Fragments of stories, woven with care,
Remind us of journeys, remind us to dare.
In the tapestry rich with the hues of our past,
We linger in places where dreams ever last.

Tapping through the Dewy Darkness

In the hush of night's embrace,
Whispers dance in misty grace.
Footsteps soft on emerald blades,
Dreams awake in twilight's shades.

Stars above in silence gleam,
Painting shadows, weaving dream.
Moonlit paths call out my name,
Guiding me through night's soft flame.

Winds carry tales from afar,
Secrets tucked in every char.
Nature's breath, a lullaby,
Tapping gently, time slips by.

Ears attuned to every sound,
In the dark, enchantments found.
As the world fades into gray,
Finding light along the way.

The Soft Glow of Enigmas Past

Memories wrapped in gentle light,
Flickers dance, soft and bright.
Echoes of forgotten days,
Guided by a golden blaze.

In the corners, shadows curl,
Whispers of the past unfurl.
Time's embrace, a tender hold,
Stories waiting to be told.

Fading photographs in frames,
Each a whisper of old names.
The heart sifts through tales well spun,
In the glow, two souls are one.

Beneath the fabric of the night,
Embers dance with subtle light.
In the stillness, find the key,
Unlocking all that's meant to be.

Ethereal Horizons of the Unknown

Veils of mist hold dreams untold,
Horizons stretch, both brave and bold.
Each dawn carries a soft sigh,
Wonders waiting, reaching high.

Beyond the realms of what we see,
Lies a world, profound and free.
Whispers beckon from afar,
Guiding hearts like northern star.

Vistas shimmer in the haze,
Charting paths through ancient ways.
Hope ignites like morning's glow,
Blazing trails where spirits flow.

In the quest for truths concealed,
Every heartache, every shield.
Leads us forth to seek and find,
Ethereal realms that bind.

Captured in a Dance of Light

Flickering flames, a waltz divine,
Hearts entwined in rhythms fine.
Every shadow, every spark,
Guides the glow within the dark.

Whirls of gold and silver beams,
Float like soft and fleeting dreams.
In the hush, the world stands still,
Love ignited by sheer will.

Melding colors, life's embrace,
Painting joy across the space.
In this dance, souls intertwine,
Capturing moments, yours and mine.

As the echoes start to fade,
Memories in hearts are laid.
Forever caught in pure delight,
We remain, a dance of light.

Whispering Silks

In the quiet of the night,
Threads of fate weave tight.
Gentle whispers twine,
Through shadows they align.

Softly rustling leaves,
A tale the heart believes.
Moonlit paths ahead,
On silken dreams we tread.

Veils of mystery flow,
In the breezes that blow.
Secrets softly shared,
In dreams we've both dared.

Every sigh a tale,
In this enchanted vale.
With each fabric spun,
A new journey begun.

Enchanted Twilight

When the day meets night,
Stars begin their flight.
A canvas painted wide,
With hopes and dreams inside.

Beneath the twilight's glow,
Softest breezes blow.
Whispers of the trees,
Carry secrets with ease.

Flickering fireflies dance,
In a delicate trance.
The world begins to rest,
In twilight, we're blessed.

Hands entwined as one,
Until the night is done.
In this magic space,
Time slows its fast pace.

Glimmering Dreamscape

In a land of silver streams,
Where reality meets dreams.
Stars like diamonds shine,
In a night so divine.

Clouds of cotton candy float,
On a soft, sweet sea boat.
Whispers of the night call,
Wake the magic in all.

Fairies dance on moonbeams,
Crafting more than it seems.
Colors swirl and blend,
In a journey without end.

Every step a delight,
In this shimmering light.
Close your eyes and see,
What your heart sets free.

Enshrouded Truths

Hidden in the shadows deep,
Lies a secret we must keep.
Words unspoken lie awake,
In the silence, hearts ache.

Truths wrapped in mystery,
Awaiting history's key.
Flickering flames reveal,
What we dare not conceal.

In the darkest hour's plight,
We'll find strength in the night.
With courage, we will seek,
The profound truth we speak.

Through the veil, we will tread,
With each word we have said.
In the light of the dawn,
A new hope will be born.

The Dance of Light and Shadow

In the dusk where shadows play,
Light weaves dreams that softly sway.
Whispers of the evening breeze,
Guide the dance among the trees.

Flickering flames, a gentle glow,
Reveal the paths that we must go.
Together they twirl, hand in hand,
A mystical duet so grand.

Upon the canvas of the night,
Stars emerge, a shimmering sight.
Echoing laughter, a fleeting spark,
Illuminates the world so dark.

In the end, the shadows yield,
To the promise of light revealed.
Harmony in every shade,
In the dance of dreams we've made.

Glistening Horizons

Morning breaks with golden rays,
Painting skies in vibrant plays.
Glistening horizons call our name,
Awakening hearts with hope's bright flame.

Waves of color brush the dawn,
Revealing paths where dreams are drawn.
Nature sings in joyful tunes,
Underneath the watchful moons.

In the distance, mountains rise,
Touched by light from azure skies.
With each step, the world expands,
Across these glistening lands.

Together we chase the light,
In every moment, pure delight.
Horizons gleam, a wondrous sight,
Guiding souls toward the bright.

Echoes of the Night

As stars whisper secrets near,
The night unfolds, calm and clear.
In shadows deep, old stories dwell,
Echoes of dreams they wish to tell.

Softly the moonbeams dance around,
In the silence, magic's found.
Each rustling leaf, a gentle sigh,
Bears witness to the night sky high.

Crickets sing their timeless song,
While fireflies flicker all night long.
Together they weave a tapestry,
Of all that is wild and free.

In this realm where time stands still,
Hearts awaken to the thrill.
Echoes linger, softly bright,
In the embrace of the night.

Shroud of Serenity

In the stillness, peace unfolds,
A gentle touch, a warmth that holds.
Wrapped in love, in soft embrace,
The world dissolves without a trace.

Whispers of the morning light,
Cascading dreams take gentle flight.
Clouds drift by in tranquil skies,
Carrying hopes and lullabies.

Every heartbeat, a tender song,
Guides our souls where we belong.
In this haven, time stands still,
Cradled in a quiet thrill.

Beneath the stars, we find our way,
In the shroud of night and day.
Serenity, a balm so sweet,
In the silence, we are complete.

Moonlit Tapestry of Secrets

In the night, whispers rise,
A tapestry woven with sighs.
Stars dance in the silver glow,
Secrets hidden, yet they flow.

Soft shadows stretch and bend,
As dreams and reality blend.
In the hush, the heart can hear,
Moonlit truths, crystal clear.

Lost in time, moments gleam,
Weaving fate like a dream.
Underneath the watchful moon,
Mysteries hum a gentle tune.

Each thread bears a silent name,
In the fabric, stillness claims.
All the tales the night can weave,
In this tapestry, hearts believe.

A Shimmering Cloak of Mystery

Veiled in twilight, shadows creep,
A cloak of secrets, silence deep.
Every glimmer hides a tale,
In its folds, truth may prevail.

Stars twinkle in the hidden seams,
Whispers float like fragile dreams.
What lies beneath the shining crest?
A world where the unknown rests.

Glimmers beckon, softly call,
Each step can lead to rise or fall.
Encased in mystery's embrace,
The heart finds solace in this space.

Beneath the cloak, stories intertwine,
In every shimmer, a sign.
Life dances in the night's embrace,
Under mystery's gentle trace.

Threads of Celestial Satin

Celestial satin, soft and bright,
Threads of stars in the velvet night.
Each shimmer holds a quiet dream,
Woven stories in the moonbeam.

A tapestry spun from ancient lore,
In every strand, journeys explore.
The universe whispers, secrets unfold,
In the deep canvas, wonders told.

Glistening moments, time doth weave,
In embraced silence, we believe.
Threads connect hearts from afar,
Guided by a distant star.

Every twilight, a tale is spun,
In the glow of the evening sun.
Each weave a journey, a sacred path,
In celestial satin, destiny hath.

Reflections Beneath the Luminous Shroud

Beneath the shroud of light divine,
Reflections dance, a sacred line.
Silhouettes whisper soft and low,
In the glow where dreams do flow.

The night unveils its gentle grace,
Upon the stillness, a soft embrace.
Each star a mirror, truths displayed,
In the luminance, fears allayed.

Amidst the shadows, peace takes flight,
Guided by the softest light.
In silence, we find our way,
Underneath the night's ballet.

Every ripple, a story shared,
In the stillness, we are bared.
With every heartbeat, we are drawn,
To the warmth of the coming dawn.

Echoing Hues of Subtlety

Whispers dance in gentle shades,
Color fades in twilight's embrace.
Dreams entwined in velvet glades,
Time slows down, a tender chase.

Shadows play in emerald light,
Softly hum the twilight song.
The heart beats with pure delight,
In echoes where we all belong.

Raindrops form a crystal breeze,
Painting skies with silent grace.
Nature sighs with tranquil ease,
In the softening, sacred space.

Every brush of pastel hue,
Calls to souls both far and near.
In stillness, beauty shines anew,
A canvas born from whispered cheer.

Veils Woven from Starlit Dreams

In fields of silver, wishes flow,
Veils of night drape softly low.
Stars awaken, twinkling bright,
Weaving tales in fleeting light.

Moonbeams glisten on the stream,
Echoing every silent theme.
Each moment wrapped in ethereal,
Spinning magic, so surreal.

With every breath, the cosmos sings,
Voices rise on celestial wings.
In the hush, the heart can feel,
The universe begins to heal.

Dreams collide in cosmic play,
As dusk transforms to silver gray.
Veils of wonder, soft and sweet,
Guide us where the starlit meet.

Brushing Against the Mystical Glow

In shadows cast by softest light,
A glow emerges, pure and bright.
Whispers of the night unfold,
Stories woven, yet untold.

Glimmers flicker, silent calls,
Starlit paths through ancient halls.
The heart walks on clouds of dreams,
Lost in the warmth of moonlit beams.

Every brush of light we feel,
Carries a truth, wondrously real.
Magic dances in our view,
Painting life in vibrant hue.

As we wander through the night,
Embraced by the mystical light.
Every moment begins to glow,
Painting love in ebb and flow.

In the Realm of Shimmering Haze

Through the mist, a path appears,
Lifting dreams beyond our fears.
Softly wrapped in shades of night,
Echoes whisper of pure light.

Waves of shimmer gently swell,
Each heartbeat tells a secret spell.
Hearts awaken, spirits rise,
In the warmth of endless skies.

Every breath is filled with grace,
In this timeless, sacred space.
Wandering souls begin to chase,
The sparkling glimmers we embrace.

In the realm where shadows fade,
Beauty blooms, unafraid.
Embers glow in twilight's hand,
We find ourselves, as planned.

A Dance Beneath the Lustrous Veil

In moonlit grace, we twirl and sway,
Beneath the stars, where shadows play.
The gentle breeze whispers our names,
In this soft night, love's fire flames.

With every step, we lose the night,
Our hearts entwined, a pure delight.
The world fades away, just us two,
In the lustrous veil, dreams come true.

Through vibrant dreams, we'll softly glide,
In every heartbeat, we confide.
The universe wraps us in its arms,
Protecting us with all its charms.

As twilight fades, our spirits rise,
In the fading light, calm sighs.
A story spun, forever to tell,
In love's embrace, we dance so well.

Shadows Embrace the Glowing Front

In the twilight where shadows fall,
A glowing front begins the call.
The whispers of night, so soft and sweet,
Guide every soul on this journey fleet.

Wrapped in dusk, the world feels near,
Every echo, a voice we hear.
With every flicker, hope ignites,
As shadows embrace the upcoming lights.

The darkness dances, a soothing song,
In the depths, we find where we belong.
With every heartbeat, the night unfolds,
A tapestry of stories told.

Together we walk, hand in hand,
Through shadows deep, across the land.
A glowing front, our future bright,
In shadows' arms, we find the light.

Gleaming Horizons of the Unspoken

Beyond the hills where sunlight gleams,
Lie horizons spun from silent dreams.
With every breath, the air feels light,
A canvas vast, painted with night.

Each whisper carried on gentle winds,
Holds the secrets of where the heart begins.
In the quiet space, our souls align,
Gleaming horizons, love's design.

The stars above guide every thought,
In this stillness, we find what's sought.
With open hearts, we venture far,
To realms unknown, under every star.

In unspoken words, our spirits soar,
Through gleaming realms, we seek for more.
Together we'll chase what fate has spun,
As horizons gleam, our journey's begun.

A Tangle of Hidden Radiance

Beneath the layers, where shadows play,
Lies hidden radiance, bright as day.
In tangled paths, our spirits weave,
The truth emerges, we dare believe.

In silent corners, the whispers bloom,
Radiating light, dispelling gloom.
With every step, we venture near,
To unearth wonders, hold them dear.

In each embrace, a spark ignites,
Revealing dreams in the darkest nights.
A tangle of love, so deep yet free,
In hidden corners, you and me.

As dawn arrives, we find our way,
Unraveling threads of yesterday.
In radiant hues, we rise and shine,
In this tangled web, your heart is mine.

Mystic Tapestry

Threads of silence weave the night,
Whispers dance in lantern light.
Stars like stories, old and deep,
In the fabric, secrets sleep.

Dreams entwined with shadows tall,
Underneath the moon's soft call.
Colors blend, the past unfolds,
A tapestry of tales retold.

Winds of change will softly sweep,
Carrying the echoes steep.
Mystery in every seam,
Life's a woven, waking dream.

Sable Mist

Through the haze, shadows play,
Sable mists hide the day.
Whispers brush against my cheek,
In the dark, the lost heart seeks.

Underneath the quiet shade,
Secrets linger, memories fade.
Haunting calls from deep within,
Guided by the night's soft sin.

Veils of darkness gently weave,
In their depths, we learn to breathe.
Silken fog, a lover's kiss,
Wrapped in dreams, we find our bliss.

Chasing Moonbeams

I run beneath the silver sky,
To catch the light that floats on high.
Moonbeams dance on waves that sigh,
With every leap, I feel I fly.

Through the night, my heart's ablaze,
Chasing shadows, lost in a haze.
Glimmers twirl in a playful race,
Each soft glow, a sweet embrace.

In the stillness, dreams take form,
Guided by the night's soft charm.
With every step, the world anew,
Chasing dreams that feel so true.

Woven Illusions

In the twilight's dusky glow,
Woven tales begin to flow.
Each thread holds a secret bright,
Illusions formed in fading light.

Crafted visions, bold and grand,
Dancing softly, hand in hand.
Layers deep, they twist and turn,
In their heart, the embers burn.

Entangled in a web of grace,
Time slips into its soft embrace.
Here, reality meets the dreams,
In woven paths, life often deems.

Luminous Whispers

In the night where stars collide,
Softly glows a hidden tide.
Gentle echoes, hearts ablaze,
Whispers weave through moonlit haze.

Secrets dance on silver beams,
Carried forth in fragile dreams.
Every blink, a tender sigh,
Luminous, the nights drift by.

Voices murmur through the trees,
Rustling leaves, a ghostly breeze.
Hope ignites in darkened skies,
As the dawn begins to rise.

Hold the whispers close, dear friend,
In their warmth, our souls transcend.
Light the path with every thought,
In each moment, love is sought.

Ethereal Gossamer

In the dawn, where colors blend,
Threads of light begin to mend.
Fragile webs of pastel light,
Ethereal dreams take flight.

Softly woven in the air,
Gossamer whispers, light as fare.
Nature's art, a painter's grace,
In this realm, a sacred space.

Every sigh a shimmering lace,
Traces left in time and space.
Gliding through the morning dew,
A world reborn, fresh and new.

Embrace the magic, let it flow,
In the light, let spirits grow.
Together, we shall always find,
Ethereal threads that bind.

Shimmering Secrets

Hidden deep in twilight's fold,
Shimmering secrets yet untold.
Every glint a story spun,
In the shadows, dreams are won.

Glimmers dance on water's face,
Whispers soft in nature's grace.
Hushed confessions, light bestowed,
In the night, our hearts are owed.

Flickers of a distant flame,
Every glance might bear a name.
Unraveled truths beneath the stars,
Illuminate our hidden scars.

Shimmer bright when darkness nears,
Hold the secrets, calm your fears.
In the silence, find your sight,
Shimmering in the depths of night.

Glistening Shadows

Beneath the trees where shadows dwell,
Glistening stories start to swell.
Every rustle, every sound,
Whispers rise from sacred ground.

Flickers of light through branches glide,
Secrets linger, hearts collide.
In the dusk, the colors blend,
Glistening paths that never end.

Echoes of a time gone by,
Softly breathing, a gentle sigh.
In the shadows, souls entwine,
Glistening threads of the divine.

Trust the night, embrace the dark,
In the shadows, find the spark.
Every glimmer, just a clue,
Glistening light will guide us through.

Whispered Echoes

In shadows where secrets dwell,
Voices rise and softly swell.
They weave through time, a gentle stream,
Carrying whispers, a fading dream.

Beneath the stars, they lightly twist,
A sigh of night, an unseen tryst.
Each echo lingers, a haunted trace,
In the vastness of this space.

They dance around with tender grace,
Echoing love in soft embrace.
Invisible threads of laughter shared,
In every heart, a song declared.

Through corridors of the mind they roam,
Whispered echoes, a route to home.
In silent moments, they find their way,
Revealing what words can't say.

Mists of Eternity

In the dawn where shadows creep,
Mists of time begin to weep.
Veil of dreams, both soft and light,
Cloaking secrets from the sight.

Each tendril holds a tale untold,
Of fleeting moments, treasures bold.
Wandering paths in silence cry,
Whispers of those who once passed by.

The faintest breath of memory glows,
Like petals kissed by morning's rose.
In mists, the world starts to fade,
A canvas where new dreams are made.

Eternity swirls in soft embrace,
An endless dance, a timeless place.
Through shifting veils, we search and see,
The images of what will be.

Dappled Light

Through the leaves, the sunlight plays,
Casting shadows in a maze.
Dancing flickers on the ground,
Nature's whispers all around.

With every shift, a new delight,
Golden hues in gentle flight.
A symphony of warm embrace,
Illuminating nature's grace.

In the forest, we find our way,
Guided by the light of day.
Each dappled beam a soft caress,
Reminding us we are blessed.

Underneath the boughs so high,
We marvel at the vast blue sky.
In each glow, a story told,
With dappled light, the world unfolds.

Lattice of Dreams

In twilight hours, where dreams entwine,
A lattice grows, a design divine.
Each thread a wish, each knot a hope,
We weave our stories, learn to cope.

Under starlit skies, we dare to soar,
Through the lattice, we seek for more.
Carving paths with thoughts so bright,
Illuminating the endless night.

Linked in purpose, hearts aligned,
In this tapestry, we find.
A universe within our grasp,
A dance of souls, an endless clasp.

In whispered tones, our dreams embrace,
A lattice of love, a sacred space.
Together we rise, together we gleam,
Bound by the magic of a dream.

Gossamer Threads of Distant Whispers

In twilight's hue, they softly gleam,
Like shadows tangled in a dream.
A dance of voices, faint and bright,
Weaving stories in the night.

Through silver leaves, the breezes sigh,
As echoes of the past drift by.
Each murmur carries soft intent,
A tapestry of what was meant.

Along the paths where memories flow,
The gentle winds begin to blow.
They speak of love and tales once spun,
In gossamer threads, our hearts are one.

So listen close, beneath the stars,
The whispers travel near and far.
In every breath a promise lies,
In gossamer wisps, we still arise.

Shining Echoes of the Forgotten

Faded faces in the light,
Holding secrets, pure and bright.
They dance within the shadows cast,
Whispers of a time long past.

Echoes linger in the air,
Carried on a breeze so rare.
Every heart retains the beat,
Of stories lost, yet bittersweet.

In distant halls, they laugh and cry,
With memories that never die.
Their glow ignites the night's embrace,
In shining echoes, we find grace.

So let us heed their call anew,
For in their glow, we'll find what's true.
No memory fades, no story small,
In shining echoes, we recall.

Luminous Draperies of the Past

Woven threads of gold and grace,
Draping time in warm embrace.
Each flutter tells a tale of yore,
In luminous shades, we seek for more.

From ancient halls to silent glades,
Their beauty lingers, never fades.
The past unfolds its gentle hand,
In luminous drapes, we understand.

Where whispered thoughts and dreams convene,
In every fold a cosmic scene.
The past alights with vibrant hue,
In draperies, our visions brew.

So let us wander through the seams,
Where memory lives, and hope redeems.
In luminous threads, we find our way,
Through fabric woven in the day.

Enshrouded in Mystical Light

Veils of mystery softly swirl,
In silence, ancient visions unfurl.
Stars embrace the twilight's dance,
Enshrouded in a fleeting chance.

Where shadows play and whispers fall,
A world awakened by a call.
Mystical light transcends the night,
Enfolding dreams in silver white.

With every breath, the night ignites,
A symphony of gentle flights.
In twilight's arms, we softly glide,
Enshrouded, where our hopes reside.

So take my hand and close your eyes,
Together we'll unveil the skies.
In mystical glow, we'll find our truth,
Enshrouded in a dance of youth.

Hazy Wreaths of Shining Night

In twilight's tender, gentle kiss,
Hazy wreaths of stars drift by.
Whispers of dreams in fleeting bliss,
Beneath a vast and velvet sky.

Moonlight dances on waves so sheer,
Silken threads of night unwind.
Each moment captured, crystal clear,
Adrift in echoes, softly blind.

Shadows twine with secrets told,
As night weaves tales of old despair.
Wreathed in silver, they unfold,
Cascades of time in midnight air.

In every sigh, the darkness sings,
A lullaby for hearts that ache.
Hazy wreaths of nighttime flings,
Embrace the dreams that life could make.

Echoes of a Distant Silver Glow

Across the fields, the echoes play,
A distant silver glow appears.
Illuminating paths of gray,
Awakening forgotten years.

With every shimmer, shadows dance,
Imagined whispers on the breeze.
Caught in a spiral, lost in chance,
The world relents and bends its knees.

Glimmers of hope in twilight's breath,
Invite the weary to take flight.
In fleeting moments, life and death,
Merge in the endless, starry night.

As silver echoes softly fade,
The heart remembers what it knows.
In twilight's grasp, dreams are laid,
Within the pull of night's warm glow.

Chasing Ethereal Reflections

In stillness, dreams reflect the stars,
Chasing whispers through the night.
Each thought a journey, near and far,
In depths of dark, they seek the light.

Mirrors of time glint with secrets,
Fragments of life begin to weave.
Through the haze of doubt and regrets,
We chase the truth, we seek, believe.

Thoughts flicker, like fireflies bright,
Ethereal moments, fleeting grace.
In their glow, we find our flight,
Lost in the dance, we find our place.

Chasing echoes of our own dreams,
Beneath the trees, the shadows play.
In every breath, the wonder gleams,
As night unveils the light of day.

The Forgotten Texture of Light

In the quiet, memories bloom,
Forgotten texture drapes the dawn.
Golden threads emerge from gloom,
A tapestry of hope is drawn.

Fingers trace the paths of days,
In every shadow, warmth resides.
Patterns etched in sunlit rays,
Where dreams and reality collide.

The heart remembers colors bright,
Vivid hues in faded frames.
Rekindled spark in morning light,
Reveals the beauty of our names.

With every shift, reflections gleam,
The forgotten whispers of delight.
Weaving through the fabric of dream,
Eternal dance — the texture of light.

Luminescent Signs of Untold Tales

Beneath the stars, whispers sigh,
Echoes of stories, drifting high.
Their glow reveals what's long been lost,
In twilight's grasp, we count the cost.

Flickers of hope in shadowed nooks,
The finest ink in battered books.
Each spark a tale waiting to be told,
Of dreams once bright, now fading gold.

Along the paths of wandering hearts,
These signs remind us, life imparts.
Through restless nights, we seek their light,
Guiding us onward, through the night.

In every glimmer, truths entwined,
A symphony of the undefined.
In the silence, secrets grow,
Luminescent tales begin to flow.

Whispering Echoes Through Dull Curtains

In quiet rooms where shadows dwell,
The air is thick, a muted shell.
Whispers curl like smoke and sigh,
Silent tales that float and fly.

Dull curtains hide the past and pain,
Fading echoes of love's refrain.
Through fabric worn, they slip and dance,
Inviting hearts to take a chance.

Softly they weave, a tender thread,
Of whispered dreams and words unsaid.
In the dim light, secrets wait,
For courage found to open fate.

So peel back layers, feel the sway,
Let echoes guide you on your way.
In whispered tones, life's truths unfold,
Through dull curtains, stories bold.

The Mist of Hidden Radiance

In morning light, a veil descends,
The world transformed, as day begins.
A fog of dreams, both soft and bright,
Concealing rays of hidden light.

Within the mist, lost hopes reside,
Where ancient wishes quietly bide.
They shimmer faintly, waiting still,
For hearts to break the quiet chill.

Each breath releases what was thought,
A chance for dreams that time forgot.
In every whisper, a spark ignites,
A realm of wonder, new delights.

As sunlight pierces through the haze,
The hidden realms begin to blaze.
In paths unwalked, the heart must roam,
To find the light that leads us home.

Silvered Glints of Enigmatic Journeys

Upon the road where starlight gleams,
Are silver glints of shrouded dreams.
They call us forth, their whispers sway,
Through rugged trails, we lose our way.

In every step, a tale unfolds,
Of daring hearts and spirits bold.
With each glint found beneath the skies,
We chase the truth in nature's guise.

The compass spins, yet still we seek,
The silver threads that softly speak.
In moments fleeting, paths collide,
A tapestry of hope and pride.

Through enigmatic journeys vast,
We gather stories from the past.
In every glint, a world ignites,
A map of wonder, guiding lights.

Horizon of Veiled Stars

The night unfolds its velvet hue,
A canvas draped in cosmic grace.
Distant worlds in silence gleam,
While shadows dance in soft embrace.

Whispers of the twilight breeze,
Carry secrets from afar.
Each flicker holds a promise bright,
A dream beneath the watching star.

The moon beholds our silent sighs,
As constellations weave their lore.
In this realm where wishes float,
The heart beats loud, yet asks for more.

Guided by the gentle night,
We wander where the starlight flows.
In this place of hope and fear,
The horizon beckons, softly glows.

The Glistening Drift of Time

Moments weave like golden threads,
In the tapestry of our days.
Countless joys and fleeting pains,
All adorned in time's embrace.

A river flows with shimmering light,
Each ripple tells a tale untold.
As sunbeams dance upon the waves,
Memories blossom, dreams unfold.

The clock ticks on, a steady beat,
Marking rhythms of the heart.
With every hour, a chance to change,
To find new paths, a brand new start.

In this drift, we find our peace,
Amidst the chaos, breath and sighs.
With open arms, we greet the dawn,
And in its light, our spirit flies.

Whispers Caught in Silken Ties

In the hush where shadows dwell,
Soft voices weave like silk and lace.
Each murmur carries tender notes,
A melody to fill the space.

Beneath the veil of secrets kept,
Hearts entwined, our stories blend.
Each touch ignites a thousand stars,
In this dance where dreams transcend.

The night holds close our whispered thoughts,
A gentle breeze to hold us near.
With every sigh, a thread is spun,
A tapestry of love sincere.

Caught in bonds of delicate trust,
We reach for what tomorrow brings.
In the silence, we have found,
The magic that true longing sings.

Veiled Realms of the Twilight

As daylight fades, the colors blend,
A gentle hush, the world transforms.
In twilight's arms, illusions play,
Where fantasy and hope conform.

The horizon blushes, secrets bloom,
In shades of purple, gold, and gray.
The stars awaken, one by one,
To light the path for dreams astray.

In the stillness, silence speaks,
Tales of shadows, lost in time.
Each heartbeat resonates with fate,
As echoes turn to whispered rhyme.

We wander through this mystic haze,
Where dusk and dawn and night align.
In veiled realms, we find our place,
A sanctuary, yours and mine.

Secrets Drift Through the Moonlit Mist

Whispers in the evening air,
A gentle breeze that stirs the night.
Stars above begin to glare,
As shadows dance in silver light.

Veils of fog embrace the trees,
Softly hiding what's concealed.
A hush unfolds upon the breeze,
With mysteries that are revealed.

Footsteps fade upon the ground,
Echoes of what once was said.
In the stillness, secrets found,
In the quiet, words are bred.

Underneath the moonlit gaze,
Dreams and whispers intertwine.
In this realm where silence plays,
Secrets drift, ethereal, divine.

Woven Light of Secrets Unseen

Threads of light in the tapestry,
Stitched together, bold yet fine.
Every strand holds the mystery,
Of a truth both dark and divine.

In shadows where the stories keep,
The woven tales begin to glow.
Unraveling secrets buried deep,
Among the whispers, soft and slow.

Flickers of truth in twilight's weave,
Patterns that flicker, fade, and blend.
In each design, a tale we leave,
An unbroken line that won't bend.

Beneath a quilt of starlit skies,
Rests the essence of dreams untold.
With every stitch, a thousand sighs,
In woven light, our secrets fold.

Glinting Threads of Twilight Truth

As twilight casts its gentle hue,
Glimmers spark the fabric's fold.
Threads of truth arrayed anew,
In whispers low, stories unfold.

Each glint a moment caught in time,
The echoes of the day's last breath.
Weaving tales, a silent rhyme,
A dance with shadows, life and death.

In the canvas of fading light,
Secrets shimmer, hidden gems.
Echoes whisper through the night,
Revealing what the heart condemns.

Captured in the twilight's grasp,
Every spark ignites the dark.
In fragile threads, our truths clasp,
Glinting softly, leaving their mark.

Hiding in a Sheen of Subtlety

A sheen rests upon the surface,
Beneath the calm, a world lies still.
Veiled whispers hold a quiet purpose,
In shadows cast, emotions spill.

Subtle hints in the passing breeze,
A thread of grace, a delicate sigh.
In the stillness, time seems to freeze,
As softness drapes like a gentle lie.

Layers deep, a mystery grows,
In the fabric where silence reigns.
A hidden truth nobody knows,
In the quiet, life refrains.

Beneath the surface, secrets dwell,
In a sheen of natural grace.
With every glance, a silent spell,
Where subtlety finds its place.

Celestial Drapery

Stars shimmer in the night air,
Whispers of dreams dance with care.
Clouds drape softly over the sky,
Celestial wonders drift and sigh.

The moon, a lantern, glows so bright,
Casting shadows in the gentle night.
Galaxies swirl in a velvet sea,
Mysteries wrapped in tranquility.

Each twinkle tells a tale untold,
Of ages past and secrets old.
In the hush of night, we find our place,
Underneath the stars' embrace.

And as dawn breaks, dreams take flight,
Fading shadows greet the light.
Yet the memories of stars remain,
Celestial drapery, joy and pain.

Moonlit Enigma

Under the moon's soft glow,
Silhouettes move, quiet and slow.
Mysteries linger in the air,
A secret held with tender care.

The night whispers with silken tone,
Each shadow cast, a story sown.
The path is veiled in silver light,
Leading hearts through the deep of night.

In the stillness, time stands still,
As echoes of dreams begin to fill.
Every glance holds a whispered plea,
In the moonlit dance, we are free.

Yet dawn will break, and truths will spark,
Illuminating the hidden dark.
For every enigma has its rhyme,
In the tapestry of space and time.

Radiant Mist

Morning breaks with a gentle kiss,
Veils of fog wrap in quiet bliss.
Radiant light spills, soft and warm,
A tender touch after the storm.

Mist rises slowly, the world anew,
Colors blending, a vibrant hue.
Nature's brush, so deft and fine,
Creating magic, a grand design.

Each droplet shines like a gem so rare,
Suspended moments hang in the air.
In this silence, we find our peace,
As the beauty of morning will never cease.

With every breath, the day unfolds,
In the radiant mist, life beholds.
An orchestra of light and sound,
In this tender dawn, love is found.

Veiled Reflections

In the mirror's gaze, we meet our fate,
Shadows whisper, secrets await.
Veiled reflections dance with grace,
Echoes of truth in a quiet space.

Hazy memories flicker bright,
Painted moments, lost in light.
Each glance reveals a story spun,
Of battles fought and victories won.

Beneath the surface, depths reside,
Fragments of self we often hide.
Yet courage blooms where shadows dwell,
In veiled reflections, we know ourselves well.

And when the light begins to fade,
The stories linger, never betrayed.
For in every heart, a mirror stays,
Veiled reflections of our days.